Vietnam
And Other Heartaches

Vietnam
And Other Heartaches

Peter C. Fraser,
Major-US Army Retired

iUniverse, Inc.
New York Lincoln Shanghai

Vietnam and Other Heartaches

Copyright © 2007 by Peter C. Fraser

All rights reserved. No part of this book may be used or reproduced by any means, graphic, electronic, or mechanical, including photocopying, recording, taping or by any information storage retrieval system without the written permission of the publisher except in the case of brief quotations embodied in critical articles and reviews.

iUniverse books may be ordered through booksellers or by contacting:

iUniverse
2021 Pine Lake Road, Suite 100
Lincoln, NE 68512
www.iuniverse.com
1-800-Authors (1-800-288-4677)

ISBN-13: 978-0-595-39436-4 (pbk)
ISBN-13: 978-0-595-83833-2 (ebk)
ISBN-10: 0-595-39436-1 (pbk)
ISBN-10: 0-595-83833-2 (ebk)

Printed in the United States of America

This book is dedicated to the men and women of the Armed Forces who serve on today's battlefields in Iraq and Aphganistan. A special salute to today's young Rakkasans of the 101st Airborne. Those of us who went before you, we will not let America forget your service. Your gallantry inspires America.

This book is dedicated to the 168 young men of the 3d Battalion, 187th Infantry, Third Brigade of the 101st Airborne Division who died in combat operations in 1967–1968, my year in Vietnam. To my comrades in arms whose valor was so common place during that year we fought together, we must never forget the cost of freedom. That cost is the shattered lives, the blood and sweat, the tears and dreams, all the things that young people surrendered then, and continue to sacrifice today for the ideal and the belief in what is America.

I also wish to express my appreciation to Julie Stieskel and Congressman Tim Ryan whose encouragement and support got me to share this poetry with America.

Finally there are many that gave me encouragement and guidance as I worked to get this book ready to publish. Francine Arroyo who proofed many of my poems and Mrs. Dennis Malaski, my favorite English teacher, who corrected my grammar. My daughter, Emily, for designing the cover. Finally to my fellow veterans who shared many of their experiences with me in an attempt to find peace. Some of what you shared is here on these pages along with my own. America needs to know the cost she exacted from you over the past 30 years.

A special thanks to Earl R. Van Alstine of Elkridge, MD, for his permission to use the photograph on the front cover. The photo, taken by Earl, is of Kenny Kotyluk shortly before he was killed in action providing medical aide to wounded members of the Battalion in 1968. Not a day goes by that I do not think of him and the others who died that year serving this nation.

Contents

Vietnam and Other Heartaches 1
Good Morning Vietnam 2
Angel of the Morning 3
The Black and White of Dying 4
Billy Turner 5
Ap Trang Dau 7
C-Ration Blues 9
Air Strike 10
Busting Bush 11
Firefight 12
Back Home 13
Fear 14
Tracers 15
War's Reality 16
Song Be River 17
Nurses 19
Point Man 21
Jungle Trail 22
Montagnard Village 23
Griffin 24
Friendly Fire 25
Charlie Cong 26
Body Count 27

Air Support	28
Listening Post	29
Phouc Vinh Bunker	30
Buying the Farm	31
Stars and Stripes	32
Combat	33
Cu Chi	34
Dear Mr. Cronkite	35
Day to Day Crap	36
Tracer Thoughts	37
Dinkee Dau	38
Ebbing Life	39
Fear and Frustration	41
Foxholes	42
Kenny	43
My Admired Enemy	44
Night Battle	46
Mail Call	48
Right Hand Man	49
Prather	50
Old Two Step	51
Care Package	52
Tet 68	53
The Night	54
DEROS	55
Forever Nineteen	56
Anniversary Date	57
Wondering	58
Incoming	59

My Wall	60
The Lieutenant's Eulogy	61
Line in the Sand	63
Desert Crossroads	64
Brothers	66
Boots on the Ground	67
For Jessica Lynch	69
For a Soldier Lost in Combat	71
Iraqi Casualty	72

Vietnam and
Other Heartaches

Good Morning Vietnam

Good morning, Vietnam.
Our door gunner sprays the jungle
while Cobra makes it's run;
spitting death from its cannon,
it sends two 40mm rockets into the jungle.
Then the Hueys clap, clap, clap into the LZ
as air support drops down out of the sky
putting napalm into the jungle.
Puff sprays a hailstorm of death
prepping the AO for our insertion.
Fear grips your stomach;
your balls feel like they are in your belly;
as your Huey nears the ground
and you exit into the unknown.
What a way to greet the early morning sun
as you start another day of fighting and dying.
Firefight to firefight, time suspended by fear,
you search and destroy.
Through the heat of the day you push on
just trying to survive the day.
Finally it is over,
the quiet returns for a little while.
You relax with your buddies,
killing what's left of the day,
before having to do it all over again tomorrow.

Angel of the Morning

Out in the bush on foot patrol,
busting the bush, crossing rice paddies.
The word came from the Lt.,
take five, we got a break.
Dennis Moore breaks out his radio.
Armed Forces Radio is here with us.
It is our only contact with the real world.
Fifteen guys in a rice paddy
huddled around a transistor radio.
We listen as Merrilee Rush
sings *"Angel of the Morning."*
For a couple of moments
round eyed girls and back home fills our thoughts.
Then as combat-weary GI's do,
we told stories of those back home girls
and the good times we never had.
Stories about the touchdown pass almost caught,
the fast cars we almost bought,
and the backseat girls who never came through.
We were killing time and wishing we were all back in the real world.
The war seems gone, half-forgotten for a brief moment.
We escape the fighting and the dying
still aware that this is our ever-present reality.
We all know the next angel we see
may well be the angel of death.

The Black and White of Dying

When I first got to Nam,
you were black and I was white.
Then sweating together
through the boonies and in firefights
we became brothers.
Everything we did depended on each other.
Without speaking, we communicated.
I knew if I went left,
you would go right.
to be there to cover me in a firefight.
I never trusted another person
as I trusted you.
We became as one.
When you got hit,
a part of me felt your pain.
A part of me went with you on the dustoff,
a part of me died with you,
and a part of me is still with you.
Your memory gives me the strength
to go on with the day to day of living.
But at night,
when dreams come calling,
you are there, forever young.

Billy Turner

I remember the courage of your dying.
Time will not take away the details
of where we were and what you did.
What I recall most was how you died.

Some may say you died in vain,
but they did not have the privilege of your smile.
Nor did they know the value we placed on each other
to do what had to be done.

No man could hold in his heart
the love I have for you,
For I have never shared as much of myself
as I did with you.

When we walked the Valley of Death
we formed a bond of faith.
I could demand of you what I did of myself,
knowing you would not falter.

When you died so others could live,
I never called you a hero.
But today, after so many years, I find you still with me
A man among men whose memory I will never let die.

Your valor is known beyond the grave,
not on a monument, which I would build if I could,
but in my spoken word shared with others
too young to have known our battles.

In our youth, we fought a battle that took your life,
but it failed to kill your spirit,
for it lives on in my memory and in my words,
as much as it lived in your deeds.

Ap Trang Dau

Human wave.
The battle lasted not thirteen minutes,
just long enough for so many to die.
A lot of good soldiers went down that night.

Charlie is slick,
he will sneak up close and wait.
He waits until dark, then comes all at once,
five hundred strong.

Thirty-eight died
and thirty more were wounded,
left lying in the open rice paddy.
Dawkins was a medic and one of the last to go down.

Ben loved to tell drinking stories
about his rock and rye.
He loved the bamdebah
and drinking cold 33.

We had been together for over two years,
One gets to know someone in that period of time.
Just like that,
Charlie cancelled his friendship.

Captain Jenkins was the CO,
his first command and his last.
On the radio we all heard his final words
I'm a goner was what he said.

We sent them home,
far from those who knew them best,
Just more statistics in a war
where the only goal is getting home alive.

C-Ration Blues

I'm last to the C's.
All that is left
is Ham and Lima Beans.
Threw it into the jungle,
telling Old Charlie Cong he can have them.
Two seconds later, they come flying back.
A voice from the jungle
"Number ten GI,"
"you keep, Charlie no want."
The only good use for Ham and MotherFuckers
is stringing a jungle antenna.
Tie the WD-1 to the can
and throw it as high and as far as you can.
That's the only thing they are good for.

Air Strike

An incoming aircraft, a Phantom
it's engine screaming.
Two canister tumbling, dropping from the sky.
An eternity passes as they fall slowly into the jungle.
The deafening roar of the explosion
followed by the concussion.
Then the gasoline-like smell of napalm quickly fills the air.
Nobody is lighting up to smoke,
afraid we would all get blown away
should it go off.
As a grunt, I don't like seeing what it does.
It does however, truly make Charlie a believer
by turning him into a crispy critter.
Not a pretty sight.
Yet I'm grateful,
we have it and Charlie doesn't.
Makes it easy to call the sky boys
When your ass is in a bind.

Busting Bush

The hardest part of "Busting Bush"
is putting one foot in front of the other.
What has become paramount to everybody
is to keep moving.
Hungry, tired, thirsty, sweaty, dirty,
nothing else matters anymore.
Just keep moving,
a hundred pounds of death rides on your back,
claymores, M-60 rounds, M-16 ammo and 81mm mortar rounds.
All together, they make each step an act of total concentration
and co-ordination.
So loaded down, buddies push and pull each other
just to cross-streams and other obstacles.
Wearily moving until you get a break,
then you drop to the ground,
take off your ruck
and spend the next ten minutes burning leeches off.
This is the part of war that is hell.
Busting Caps ain't nothing compared to Busting Bush.
Moving from anywhere to nowhere
You wish there was an easier way to fill the time
between firefights.

Firefight

A firefight is short,
short enough to last a lifetime.
I am so callused towards death
because I know it so well.
At the same time I am scared as hell
because death now knows me.

It comes in the day.
It comes at night.
It hangs all around me.
Even my uniform smells like death.
Each time it rains, I take off my shirt
and try to wash the smell away.

The kid who died today
was only eighteen.
It seems a shame
that he will never grow old like me.
At nineteen I'm senile
and a little crazy in the head.

Back Home

Seems all that everyone talks about
is what's happening in the real world.
This ain't real,
though reality is all around us.
Everybody reads the hometown rag
because it keeps us believing
that we can get back.
This hellhole is just temporary;
home is still there waiting for us.
Stay alive, DEROS this place.
Do whatever you have to do.
Just believe in yourself,
and those guys around you.
This is my reality.
In these guys I place all my trust.
These guys are my brothers.
I trust them with my life
as they trust me with theirs.
This is all we have,
each other.

Fear

In that brief moment of not knowing,
fear can grab hold of anyone.
Fear is a creature that can possess a man's heart
and feed on his soul.
It robs the young of their innocence,
those older, of their wisdom.
In the brief seconds of a firefight a life is taken.
I watch as a boy who did the killing
is forced to become a man.
He did not understand the essence of his new self
as he had not yet matured.
He found he was at odds with what he had become.
Shackled into that manhood he does not understand
the boy inside longs to escape.
However the inescapable is within
and has become a part of him.
Unable to understand this new part of himself;
unable to cope with this turmoil and anguish,
in a firefight he stands up, he hesitates.
That way something he can not control
enables him to check out and escape

Tracers

Tracers arc through the night,
looking like fireflies, only ones that sting.
The hypnotic power entrancing and mesmerizing
as like a dancing messenger of death,
it races through the night.
Looking for someone to talk to.

War's Reality

All of the atrocities of war
are left for the living.
Only we are able to realize the full impact.
We see the child crippled, a young girl maimed.
You see, the dead enjoy the finality of death,
while we the living are haunted
by the horror of their dying.
All around us is the war.
In the rubble of a bombed-out hooch,
in the roar of a jet bombing,
the crack of a rifle shot.
We can smell it, taste it, even feel it.
It climbs into our sleep,
it fills our dreams.
It is everywhere around
until with astounding clarity it strikes.
Shit, man, we are the war.

Song Be River

Out on the water of the Song Be River,
two guys in a rubber raft.
Body hunting,
someone has drowned.

To much shit
strapped to his rucksack.
Pulled him under,
he never came up.

A hundred guys mull around,
spread out along the shore.
Each one looking at his feet,
avoiding each other's eyes, nothing to say.

Wasn't Charlie
shooting his AK-47,
or a booby trap
that took him away.

It don't really matter,
to us it was all the same.
He was just as dead
and we all felt the loss and the pain.

Captain says, *"saddle up."*
"Move the fuck out."
"First Platoon, take point."
"Third Platoon bring up the rear."
"Lets get the hell out of here."

That is the way it goes down
out here in the bush
in sunny South Vietnam.
Just another day out of your 365,
in your deluxe foot tour of "The Nam"

Nurses

One could almost taste the fear,
danger was all around us.
From the silence of the jungle
you could tell Charlie was close.
Contact.
I felt the pain but never heard a sound.
I felt a calm, the fear was gone.
Someone called "*Medic*" and help was at hand.
I got a battle dressing, then he was gone.
Some had wounds that were critical
I heard him say to the RTO, "*get a dustoff fast.*"
We were put on the chopper and carried away.
I must have drifted off; I thought I had died.
The next thing I heard was a soft, gentle voice
asking if I hurt.
Her eyes were so blue I knew she was an angel.
She went to the others, hurt worse than me.
The guy beside me, I knew he was bad.
I watched as she took him into her arms,
holding him tight as he died.
I watched her cry as she closed his eyes.
I tried to tell her I understood
but they took me away to patch up my wounds.
I never saw her again so I could tell her
I know why you cried.
I never got to thank her for being there,
for easing our pain and helping us out.
To me she will always be something special
for helping us both the living and the dead.

I have thought of her so many times
and I just want to say "*Thanks.*"
To all the nurses that fought in OR's and wards,
you really were angels to us.
I know God has a special place in heaven for you
because you went to hell for us.

Point Man

Out front moving cautiously,
all alone,
the point man puts his life on the line.

Breaking jungle and hacking through bamboo,
he sweats,
both from exertion and fear.

His quick responses keep all alive.
Alert to any danger,
life and death hang in the balance.

One man all of eighteen,
so very human, yet
all our lives depend on him.

Rifles crack, the silence broken,
firefight reactions take over,
Tracers and AK rounds fill the air.

Alive,
he is good;
Dead,
he is replaced.

Jungle Trail

Hidden in the jungle,
almost lost in the growth,
is the trail Charlie uses.

Invisible signs tell the locals
stay away and off the trail
or you will die.

Simple as that, Charlie knows
the only ones on the trail are Americans,
so he sets his booby traps.

An effective way to control the locals-
We try to win their hearts and minds,
while Charlie just scares the shit out of them.

Wonder which way is best?
I certainly know which is effective;
so I will DEROS and still not understand.

Montagnard Village

1968
High in the Central Highlands of Vietnam
in a Montagnard village,
as night settles in around us,
I listen.
Children in harmony singing.
I ask what the words mean.
They sing of a battle fought 3000 years ago.
I am struck by the irony of it all.
I am here in my own war.
I wonder if, someday a thousand years from now,
A soldier will be sitting by a fire
and he will listen to Montagnard children
and the song they sing, will it be about me?

Griffin

The warm stickiness of your blood
clings to my fingers and melts into my clothing.
I am trying so hard to hold your life inside you.
I never knew a person could bleed so much.
So much damage to a body,
one wound patched up;
I find another one oozing blood.
I work as fast as I can,
but it is just not fast enough.
I should have realized from the look on your face
you are talking with God.
So long young soldier, my brother in arms,
you just passed final muster.
Here are your discharge papers from this army,
you just joined His army in Heaven.

Friendly Fire

A two mill error for the crest of the hill
put eight rounds of artillery in the middle of our Bn NDP.
Screaming *"Check Fire"* into the radio the FO turned white.
"Eight more inbound" was all he said.
In the middle of the night so many died
from those artillery rounds;
that never made it over the hill and tore us all apart.
I found him in a hole, barely alive.
Bandages and IV's trying to keep him alive.
Screaming *"needed a dustoff"* to keep him from dying on me.
He laughed, chuckling out loud and said *"What the hell."*
Looking at me he said, *"Won't live like this"*
He closed his eyes and died.
I just held his hand, that way he does not die alone,
even though I don't even know his name.
There is no such thing as friendly fire.

Charlie Cong

Black PJ's, rubber sandals and a small bag of rice.
Fifty rounds of ammo in an old sock
and a rusted AK 47 with a broken stock.
After fighting for four days to take a hill,
that is all we found.
One dead Viet Cong,
his body half hidden in a spider hole.
Two dead GI's, three wounded.
All for one dead Charlie Cong
and a hill we left as soon as we got to the top.
Hell of a way to fight a war-
unless you plan on not winning.

Body Count

Ambush moon,
Charley Cong is out on the town.
Tripping through the bush,
he stumbles into our kill zone.
It is over in seconds.

Body count, body count,
in the Nam everybody counts bodies.
One, two, three, oops.
There's the barber, four.
Everyone gets some action when Charlie is out at night.

Air Support

When you need help,
don't call the flyboys in blue.
Air Force doesn't like to deliver on the deck.
Local deliveries are not what they do best.
Coming under 1,000 feet
lets Charlie put holes in their high-priced airplanes.
There is nothing that makes high-priced airplanes into junk
faster than bullet holes.
When you need it "danger close"
and in Charlie's back pocket,
call for the Navy flyboys.
If they can park that airplane on a carrier-deck,
then they can damn sure put the ordnance where you need it.
Chances of getting out this place are better that way.

Listening Post

NDP, we stop for the night.
Weary from humping through the day
and all the clicks we have covered.
Time to enjoy the pain
of sore feet and aching muscles.
Chopper incoming with rations, mail and ammo.
Beans and franks are a connoisseur's delight
when eaten cold with rabbit to chase em down.
Pass out fresh ammo, pack away tomorrow's rations and read your mail.
You want to have time to dig in for the night.
Then as the sky turns to a shady gray
and the sun drops behind the hill,
the Lt. says "*CO wants an LP about a click or two.*"
Suddenly everyone tries to look busy,
or tries to hide in his foxhole.
You want to disappear and not be seen.
Just don't pick me is all I say to myself
I don't want an LP where your ears try to see the night,
so when, if the shit goes down,
more often than not you go with it.

Phouc Vinh Bunker

One night in August,
while I was "pulling guard "on the perimeter.
I was on the top of a Phouc Vinh bunker,
just couple of GI's and I, shooting the shit.
Charlie started some incoming on us.
120 mm rockets and mortars
hostile as all hell,
dropping on us from the sky.
As we hugged the ground we heard the explosion.
I looked up in time to see a Huey
fireballed in the sky.
God only knows how many GI's
became MIA's that night.
We were so pissed that we spent the night
bustin caps at the village we hated with renewed intensity.

Buying the Farm

Hey, man!
Where did you go down?
The Iron Triangle or War Zone D,
maybe the trees of the Michelin,
or in the paddies outside of Cu Chi
just below the Black Virgin Mountain.
Maybe it was in the streets of Hue,
or the jungle covered mountains of Dak To.
Maybe it happened just outside of Pleiku
or down along the Song Be River.
It don't make no never mind.
Dying can come easy over here.
Like the man said about shit rolling down hill-
when you are at the bottom,
it gets you no matter what you do.
When you buy the farm over here,
you always pay in full.

Stars and Stripes

What a newspaper,
Stars and Stripes sure made us look good.
Why it made us look so damn good
is that it said we killed every "Gook" in Nam
two or three times over
the year I was in Nam.

Combat

In the pressure of combat
your senses become sensitive to everything.
They are all that stand between death and survival.
The camaraderie of facing together
the same dangers of each day,
the depending on each other to survive
builds a bond of trust.
Knowing who will do what in a firefight,
sharing hopes, dreams and frustration,
spending more time together than most do in a lifetime.
We were inseparable day and night,
we survived on each other.
After the killing, we knew never to stare.
Black body bags reduced the tension
and hid the mutilation of modern warfare
leaving us with the continued pressure of living.
Swift evacuation saved us from confronting
the sorrow, anger and frustration of someone's death.
For it took away a dead comrade,
leaving us feeling numb and empty inside.
We were forced to move on without respite.
The life and death of the war seemed to be all we had,
while the pressure builds within.

Cu Chi

In the middle of the Michelin,
where the rubber trees line up dress right,
where beautiful French villas were left
to age gracefully in the tropical sun.
The Army built a base that had an Ice Cream place
where you could get a real ice cream cone.
It was right next to the bathhouse,
where the Vietnamese girls did more than bathe you.
Cu Chi was where the most beautiful women were.
The French were very busy there.
I must have fallen in love at least three times
during my two weeks there.
Like all the other walking wounded will tell you,
Cu Chi beat the hell out of the boonies.

Dear Mr. Cronkite

Nam got us by the balls and there is no letting go.
Up is down and down is up,
until I am so drained of emotion I can feel no more.
But that's the way it goes
'til you don't exist anymore
In this hellhole, we exist to get by.
A Company took heavy casualties today
on a search and destroy mission in the Mekong Delta.
The Department of the Army sent letters to the mothers of the KIA,
but nobody sent letters to their buddies
who had to hold them as they died.
Somehow, Walter, you missed that.

Day to Day Crap

I feel sorry for myself sometimes.
Man, at times, I get downright melancholy.
Thinking back I get to remembering
and I get a feeling that is oh so sad.
For I made it out of the Nam
and I ought not to have.

Kind of hard to explain, except to another vet.
Who crawled through the rice paddies,
burnt shit, endured firefights and booby traps.
All the day to day crap and BS
that the brass dreamed up,
and we did it to keep the war in the headlines.

Tracer Thoughts

I roll over.
Pinned down on the jungle floor,
I look at the night sky.
The random flight of glowing rounds
Streak through the night's darkness.
Tracers,
Red, green, white hot,
Burning through the night.
If I were not so scared,
I might think they held a certain beauty.
In reality, they harbor death.
The grim reality of human failure
Stemming from the inability to find resolution.
So we end up killing each other
In an attempt to mask that failure.
In the end it is us on the ground,
Soldiers,
That are dying.
So here I am,
Eleven months out of high school worried about dying.
These are the thoughts the tracers give me.

Dinkee Dau

"You Dinkee Dau GI."
"You number ten."
"Five dollah, you Boom-Boom my sister?"
"She virgin."
That's the non-stop hustle line of a ten-year old Vietnamese boy.
He throws it at the fresh meat, the new guy.
His first day in country,
out bustin the bush.
Starting his 365 in the sunny south.
The Nam as it really is.
This is the bitch that once she gets you,
she never let's go.
Not until all the life gets squeezed out,
or else is blown away in a second.
With some of us,
it just takes longer.
Now or later,
in the end it don't really matter,
we all end up the same.

Ebbing Life

Where you are becomes very unimportant.
At that moment, nobody is sure of where they are going.
Young and old,
it is almost always the same.
I comforted an old mamasan who wandered into the street.
Hit by a 40mm rocket,
she lay dying and I could do nothing for her.
Beside her lies a young GI-
caught in the crossfire trying to save her.
I am bewildered seeing that strange interlude between life and death.
That moment when a smile gives way to an ashen hue,
as life ebbs, seeping through your fingers.
Their lifeblood covering the ground.
Together they lay dying,
and in dying, their blood mixes on the ground.
The old woman's grandson cries as he holds her hand.
I held the young GI's hand.
Life ebbs from them both.
Afterwards we put them into body bags.
After we put the dead GI on a chopper,
The platoon sergeant yells
'Saddle up, move out."
We start shuffling our feet,
heading out of the village,
trying to put what just happened out of our minds.
Moving on to whatever the next moment brings.

Doing anything to break death's hold on us.
We push them out of our minds,
concentrating on what we are doing
so we don't become like them.

Fear and Frustration

No soldier was ever prepared for the impact of an AK round
or the tremendous damage it did to the human body.
One was always told, "*There was nothing anyone could do
if it has his name on it.*"
What he really had to be concerned about
was the one that says "*To whom it may concern.*"
But the real irony is that, in a firefight,
he never has time to worry.
There, reaction is survival.
There is no time to think,
life and death are decided by factors
far beyond anyone's control.
This compounds the fear and the frustration
that he faces each and every day.
This is what makes war a never-ending nightmare.

Foxholes

I dig the best foxholes.
I make them long enough to lie in.
The other guys make fun of me,
digging in so deep.
They just dig down a couple of inches
so they can sit around and bullshit.
Giving me the once over,
they ask me about overhead cover.
I tell them I have that covered too.
That night, when Charlie starts dropping incoming on us,
they pile into my hole.
Then I tell them, "*Thanks*" for the overhead cover.

Kenny

Sitting here in the jungle,
holding you as you die.
Watching you die, letting you die.
Legs gone, balls gone, all wanting to live gone.
I could not have saved you.
I would not save you.
I did not save you.
The dustoff took you
but you never went away.
After you died,
you crawled so far into my mind and heart
that I still feel the ache of your dying.
Your pain stopped with your death;
my pain will stop with mine.

My Admired Enemy

Breathing hurt.
The stench of death hung in the air,
it was so overpowering.
Flies feasted on the remains
we had to count the bodies.

Last night, Charlie charged the wire.
Fearless, they never anticipated the sudden effect
of a M-16 projectile passing through their bodies.
It changes your whole outlook on things.

Now they are grotesque images of what they were,
twisted into lifeless forms that mimicked what they had been.
Soldiers of the legion of death fallen in battle,
have become the prey of an angry horde of flies.

Before we did battle,
we had mocked them in life.
Little did we realize that they bled and died
just as we did.

Now I wish to give them a soldier's burial,
for I have seen their courage
and their willingness to die
for reasons neither of us truly understood.

Perhaps in the coming of time,
as the years move aside the veil of confusion,
someone will be able to tell me
who they were that I killed on that battlefield.

Then I will be able to write
to a world that chose not to watch,
the incredible valor they showed
on that fateful night in the jungle of Vietnam.

Night Battle

Holed up in the ground,
ARVN soldiers are in their bunker firing position.
Head down and full auto,
they send as much lead as possible Charlie's way.
Using the wire to hold him up
so we could shoot him down.
Charlie's in the wire,
Nobody gets to sleep tonight.

Flares pop,
Burning white hot they light the land
Making it easier to see the VC.
Floating under a canopy of silk
it makes the night into day.
You have to realize,
as much as it makes it easy to see them,
they can also see you.

A young boy.
runs at our bunker.
He cradles a satchel charge in his arms,
so I shoot him twice in the head.
The satchel charge explodes,
now I know he is really dead.
I don't think twice about him
as another takes his place.

Midnight firefight-
flashing light from exploding grenades
highlights the sweeping tentacle of death
that is dancing from the barrel of an M-60.
Snaking around the night
it looks for Charlie Cong,
to make a believer out of him.
This all helps us make it to the morning.

In the morning,
I sit back and relax,
glad to be alive.
I dread having to clean up after Charlie.
The smell of death is everywhere.
Already the flies are covering the dead.
But in the end I realize-
better him than me.

Mail Call

Mail call is so damn special
and so very important to all of us.
Some got Snoopy letters
telling them how much they were loved
and what was waiting for them back home.
Some got letters from Mom saying "*stay safe.*"
Others letters from friends saying "*miss you.*"
For all, just for a few moments,
someone was saying you were important.
You could take your soul and nurture it-
somewhere deep inside,
away from the war,
you dared to hope you could get out of this place.
As you finished your letter,
you wanted to share it;
telling your buddies about back home,
you shared your memories,
hopes and dreams.
You gave more of yourself to them
than you had ever given anyone before.
Mail call was where the war didn't strip away your dignity
and you built the bond of brotherhood,
the bond that all who have fought share.
The common denominator of values that makes freedom real
and allows this nation to survive.

Right Hand Man

It's shit when your right hand man buys it.
Ain't right for him to check out and leave you.
Now who you gonna trust?
Who is going to cover your ass?
And how you gonna sleep
'cause you don't trust anyone enough to doze off.

Wired to the wall, I can't let go.
That would be the farm in this hellhole.
I'm just too fucking scared to die,
but I'm afraid that if I live,
I won't be able to wash away the stink of Nam
and it will be on me forever.

Where is God when you need him?
I know he has to be here somewhere.
Maybe he is just too busy,
welcoming all the guys from here
into His place in the sky.
I just hope he hasn't got a place for me yet.

Maybe I will find another right hand man.
Someone to trust so I can sleep,
someone to cover my ass when the shit hits the fan.
That way I can do the same for him.
One thing for certain,
I ain't gonna be getting up tight with him.

Prather

Prather was a cold mother.
After an ambush he would go out and get "wet."
He said it was his job
and he didn't want his men zapped
doing what he was supposed to do.

Then some REMF Butter Bar
heard he was slitting VC throats,
so he started an investigation.
Prather told them to "*Fuck Off*,"
stood up in a firefight and checked out.

Old Two Step

Bravo Company was on patrol,
strung out across the rice paddy.
That's when old two-step swam between the point man's legs.
Without hesitating, he turned,
went on rock and roll
and proceeded to blow old two-step away.
All the while Bravo, strung out as it was behind him,
got real intimate with the muck and mud.
We all knew he was dinky dau anyway.
We all got up and were able to laugh.
Nobody was hurt,
'cept old two step.
His shit was blown away.

Care Package

Got a "Care Package" out in the bush.
"Pogee Bait"
Back-home goodies in a box,
proving to me that Ohio still existed.
Even if it is your own mother,
someone does care enough
to send something that the Army has not screwed over,
it makes you realize that back home
still exists and you may just get out of this place.
Just like we shared the heat,
the jungle,
the mosquitoes,
the fear and the danger,
we shared the cookies.
Eating them fast and not wasting a crumb
so that somehow, someway,
we all got a taste of home.
That keeps us all in touch with the real world
and it gives us all the hope needed
to get through another day in this hell.

Tet 68

Got early morning patrol, beating the bush.
Walking the Nam, the deluxe foot tour of this tropical paradise
that has become our Hell.
Not today, no fighting or killing, the war is on a holiday.

Then word comes over the radio,
The holiday is over. Lock and load, shoot anything that moves.
Charlie has pulled a fast one.
Move to the LZ, choppers inbound, we are heading to Bien Hoa.

Going door to door, fighting in the streets.
Kick open a door, toss in a frag.
Spray a magazine inside, toss in another frag to be sure
before you enter the hooch, man what a rush.

Check good, cause Charlie will hide until you leave.
Then he lets you have it on the way out.
Door to door, hootch to hootch,
we just flat ass are kicking Charlie's butt.

Then three days later the back home rag is telling us
we got our asses kicked; the war ain't going to well.
All those dead were just paper kills.
Seems like such a shame wasting all those dead.

Tet 68,
We won every battle incountry,
but we didn't do so well back home.
Seems such a shame,
with so many dying like they did.

The Night

God, how I hate the night.
As twilight creeps in graying out the green
and turning the jungle black,
fear grows inside me like the winding of a clock.
Under the black cover of darkness,
the hunter becomes the hunted
and Charlie owns the night.

The fear is as real as the night;
it grips us all in it's unrelenting grasp.
Through the sleepless hours the fatigue builds,
sapping both mind and body.

In the tense haze of early morning
we lie on the jungle floor,
waiting for the warming sun
to take away the night's blanket of dark.

It is in the morning,
as the sun paints the jungle from black to green,
that you begin to relax the night's vigil
and take the countryside back from Charlie.

DEROS

Nam got us by the goads
and it keeps jerking us off.
We've been balls to the wall so damn often
I wonder if anyone else is fighting in this war.

I've seen so many firefights
and a hot LZ is the only place they put us.
I wonder if I will ever get out of this place
without the purple people eater.

Yet we go on-
not because we are good, for we surely are,
but because you can only do one day at a time
to DEROS this place.

Try to do more than that
and you get a body bag to wear home.
Everyone will get to go to your funeral,
except the buddies you left behind.

They get to keep a little bit of you
Stuck in the back of their minds.
That way you get to talk with them
if they manage to DEROS the Nam.

Forever Nineteen

Nam, 1968
I was barely old enough to shave.
I enlisted,
you were drafted right out of high school.
We spent our days patrolling the rice paddies and jungles of Nam,
while the nights were spent in a sleepless vigil.
We were together putting it all on the line.
Through the fear and the heat,
we put it all on the line.
We trusted each other with our lives.
My last memory of you was your face,
a look of total surprise,
frozen in time, locked in death,
trapped in my memory.
Never old or gray
every time I see you.
Forever nineteen.

Anniversary Date

Here it comes again.
No sleep, another sweat-filled night of tossing and turning.
Ain't no going around it or over it,
just have to go through it.
March 24, 1968,
Bien Hoa Province,
on a rain soaked night
so damn dark, you could not see.
A brief firefight, maybe a hundred rounds long.
On rock and roll that is not long at all-
just long enough to scorch my soul
with the heat of my anger.
One round and you were dead.
KIA, DOA, you were a lifeless corpse,
At eighteen, a statistic of war,
while I became a basket case.
We always made a great pair, you and I.
We still do,
On that Goddamn anniversary date.

Wondering

I often wonder
what happened to those guys,
the ones I left behind at DEROS.
Did Hamburger Hill or some unknown rice paddy
become the last thing they knew?
Or, like me, did they make it home
to ridicule and rejection.
From a powerbroker of life and death
to a has-been at twenty-one.
Sitting in bar,
I realize I've killed more men
than it takes drinks to get drunk,
so I can forget.

Incoming

It's one a.m.
and I can't sleep
'cause I'm taking incoming again.

The kids are asleep,
and their mom is too,
but I'm taking incoming again.

I toss and turn,
tearing up the bed,
because I'm taking incoming again.

The house is quiet,
the neighborhood is calm,
but I'm taking incoming again.

I sweat it out,
scared as hell,
because I'm taking incoming again.

I can't tell a soul,
no one must know,
that I'm taking incoming again.

My Wall
(On the death of Kenny Kotyluk in 1968)

It's my wall,
hard and black with the cold precision of the night.
Finding your name there made it mine.
It forms another link to the memory
of you lying in the night,
torn in two by the explosion.
Me, I was holding you together and trying to keep you alive,
while you were trying to crack jokes.
and you kept saying, *"let me die."*
It wasn't funny then and it isn't funny now,
but that was you.
Kenny, I know you know,
I never made it to California,
I never talked to your Mom;
I never told anyone.
I'm really sorry, man,
but I just got home myself.
I feel a hundred years old
and I never lived out my dreams.
I realize there is no going back,
either to Nam or my youth.
God knows I poured both into enough whiskey bottles,
only to find those empty when I was done.
Now I am dying
the slow tedious death of an old man
who has a long list of regrets
But the biggest one is
that it was you that night, not me.

The Lieutenant's Eulogy

Hey, Lt. Ruth.
Sorry I let you down.
That was real low of me.

Some of us made heaven.
Some made hell.
The rest there just ain't no telling,

Back home, some went east.
Some went west,
and some just went to pieces.

Tell you what,
when I get to feeling blue.
I head on down to D.C.

There you can see
on a solid black wall
what you already know is true.

We saw them die,
bleeding in vain,
rice paddy mud on their young faces.

Name after name,
in the order of dying.
Up there next to your name.

I know it's not much,
but it is the best I can do
standing here in the rain.

There ain't no coming back from wherever you are.
So I will tell you what.
wait for me there and I will join you.

Then we can share again the cold beer
and laugh at the dumbest things
and not be afraid of anything ever again.

But until then, at the wall,
I will just touch your name
and cry remembering you.

Line in the Sand

1991,
Thirty-three years out of the Nam.
Now I am the old war-horse, the veteran.
Everyone looks to me for something.
January 15, the first night of the war,
everyone is running around in a panic as the sirens go off.
Everyone but me, I am doing a Captain Friedrich.
Got myself a cigar and I'm in my skivvies,
standing where everyone can see me.
I am staying calm,
there is no reason to panic.
Old Saddam can't get me.
I am too miserable and ugly for him.
I figured if Charlie could not get me,
then old Saddam could not get me either.
I plan on dying an old man in bed.
I am the line in the sand.

Desert Crossroads

I stand at the crossroads of time.
Great armies across time have trod this ground.
Battles have been fought and warriors have died right where I stand.

On the horizon, a barely-rusted World War II tank.
Half-buried in the sand, serving as a sentinel,
guarding this site of historic battles.

Like a river of time, it is always the same.
The sand ebbs and flows with the wind,
The only constant is that it is always changing.

I pick up a handful of this restless sand
and try to hold in my hand,
but it escapes through my fingers.

Like a beast destined to be free,
it can not be captured
or held, even confined within my hand.

I stand and look to the horizon.
I turn, seeing yet more emptiness.
The desert stretching horizon to horizon.

There is nothing to break the monotony of its landscape.
The brown sand stretches to the sky,
as far as one can see is a vast emptiness.

The sky is a counter-balance to the sand.
It's blue contrasts the unending brown
while, here in the middle stands the warrior.

Before it's vastness I think not about dying,
or even about tomorrow.
I realize that this all can swallow you.

My significance is reduced to a mere thought.
What ever tomorrow brings,
I can do nothing about it until it is here.

Brothers

I saw myself
in the face of a young Iraqi veteran.
I knew what he had seen
and shared his pain.
A reflection of death was etched in his eyes.
Indelible, it is with him forever.
Etched into the soul of his being,
it allows him the wisdom to see
others who have lived through battle
as they really are—
Just as I was able to understand
what my uncle saw in WWII.
He knew I understood,
without words,
this shared experience
that reached across the years.
I wish that Iraqi veteran well
he has my understanding
as I have his.
The chain is unbroken
for we are its links,
and as such, we are brothers.

Boots on the Ground

Boots on the ground,
my fellow soldiers,
I am with you.

I know your fear from constant danger,
for once it was mine.
I am with you.

I know your aches from endless patrols,
for once it was mine.
I am with you.

I know your pain from flying shards of steel,
for once it was mine.
I am with you.

I know your heartbreak from comrades lost,
for once it was mine.
I am with you.

I know your desire to finish your mission,
for once it was mine.
I am with you

I know your longing to be home again,
for once it was mine.
I am with you.

I know your pride in serving this nation,
for once it was mine.
I am with you.

So come home to a welcome you have earned,
Though not mine, it will be yours.
I am with you

For Jessica Lynch

The terror of your ordeal
was our ordeal.
Your wounds will heal,
but never be confused—
war has touched your soul
and changed you forever.

You have gone into the tempest,
where few have gone, and survived.
You are stronger now, able to endure
like the sword tempered by heat.
The battle has given you strength
which only now you begin to know.

Now you are like a reed,
you can bend with the wind.
Strong enough not to break
you are resilient beyond reason.
You have given strength to us all.
This nation is stronger for your service.

You are humble enough to thank others
that carried you from your captors.
You say it was they who were brave.
Yet, each of us who are your brothers,
are as links in the chain of freedom,
we are thankful to welcome you home.

So in the middle of the night,
when memories come to call.
Remember the gallantry of those
who came in the night
and carried you to safety.
Their strength is yours now,

I take pride in your service,
just as I have pride in mine.
We add the names of those who have fallen
to the rolls of the hallowed few
who have given all in answer to duty's call.
The song of freedom is written with their blood.

For a Soldier Lost in Combat

When the breeze stirs
and gently touches my cheek,
I sense the essence of your soul.

Your worldly journey has ended,
your last battle has been fought.
I know you are in the hands of the Lord.

That is how I will think of you.
Though I may feel some sadness
for having you gone from us.

However, in my heart I can rejoice.
For I know where you are,
you can look upon the smiling face of Jesus.

So my fallen comrade,
I will forever be proud of our service,
for we have given of ourselves.

We have done what few others have
and you have earned a soldier's place of honor,
that your comrades shall always embrace.

Thus when I salute the flag,
it is you I remember,
and all whose service ended as yours.

It is your life's blood that renders the stripes so red
and your service that colors the blue,
your fidelity to America is the white.
That is why the flag is you.

Iraqi Casualty

Saw a young GI just home from Iraq yesterday.
Said "Thanks" to him for serving and being wounded over there.
Just like Nam all over again.
Young men dying and getting blown away,
without very much thought on our part for the whole process.
Seems to me that if we want our soldiers to fight for us,
the least we can do is to let him know we support him.
That way when he takes on "the bitch" in an eye-ball to eye-ball firefight
he can at least have a breakeven chance of coming home intact.
Never give politics an even chance to interfere with their young lives.
Do that, and in the end it will be like Nam and we will truly fail.
To do so will do them a grave wrong
and we veterans can never allow that.

978-0-595-39436-4
0-595-39436-1

Made in the USA
Middletown, DE
27 July 2016